Obamanomics

The Economic Policies of Barack Obama

SOME PEOPLE ONLY HAVE A FEW MINUTES TO SPARE

Minute Help Guides

Minute Help Press

www.minutehelp.com

Table of Contents

Chapter 1: How Obama Addressed a Faltering Economy

When Arizona Senator John McCain and Illinois Senator Barack Obama hit the campaign trail in 2008 in quest of the Oval Office, soon to be vacated by George W. Bush, the American economy was in crisis. The high times of the early 2000s were gone, erased by the effects of the housing market crash. The National Bureau of Economic Research reported that the American economy entered a recession, or an overall decline in economic activity, in December 2007, ensuring that the economy would surpass the wars in Iraq and Afghanistan as the primary issue on the minds of most voters.

The statistics were startling. The national debt was $1.8 trillion. Housing starts in 2008, or the number of new houses under construction, were down 45 percent from 2007. The Gross Domestic Product (GDP), which is the total dollar value of all of the goods and services produced in the U.S., decreased 3.8 percent in the last quarter of 2008, the biggest decrease since 1982. Between September and December of 2008 alone, over one and half million jobs were lost. Even Lehman Brothers, the investment banking firm that had survived railroad bankruptcies in the 1800s, two world wars, and the Great Depression could not survive the "Great Recession" and went bankrupt in September 2008, sending Wall Street and markets across the world into a panic.

On October 3, 2008, President Bush made the first major strike in federal intervention against the economic slide when he signed a $700 billion bailout package, called the Troubled Asset Relief Program (TARP) into law. TARP funds, which were later reduced to $475 billion, were intended to keep Wall Street and the nation's banks viable. A strong proponent of this bailout was Senator Obama, who made calls to his fellow Democrats in Congress on its behalf and said it was necessary to prevent massive job loss and the bankruptcy of businesses across the country.

It was a theme that Obama revisited several times in the first two years of his presidency. Riding a wave of disgust with the status quo, Obama handily defeated McCain in the election, earning more than twice the electoral votes. However, it was clear that Americans expected Obama, who ran under the slogan, "Yes, We Can," to address the struggling economy immediately. As Michael Grabell, author of "Money Well Spent?" said, **"In almost every recession and economic downturn that we have had in this country, some stimulus effort in some way was tried. And the idea is the government has the ability that maybe the private sector doesn't have: to borrow money and stimulate the economy."**

Obama implemented several pieces of legislation in an attempt to fix the economy. The American Recovery and Reinvestment Act of 2009, better known as the "stimulus package," is the most expensive and broadest action that he took, but it was not the only one. Obama was also faced with a collapsed housing market and a broken mortgage system, which most experts blame for creating the recession, as well as an auto industry on the verge of bankruptcy. In the background was a desire to live up to his own campaign promise of supporting renewable energy and creating "green jobs." The president did address all of these issues, with varying success.

Chapter 2: The American Recovery and Reinvestment Act (The Stimulus Package)

The Birth of the Stimulus Package

The amount of money spent on the American Recovery and Reinvestment Act (ARRA) is more than the Manhattan Project, which resulted in the atomic bomb, and more than the Works Progress Administration, which created roads, buildings, parks, art, and along with it, nearly eight million jobs during the Great Depression. It cost more to implement ARRA than it cost to put Neil Armstrong on the moon. ARRA is more expensive than the Marshall Plan, which rebuilt Europe after World War II, and it cost more than the war in Iraq between the years 2003 to 2010.

Before Obama ever set foot in the White House as president of the United States, he and his top advisors met in December 2008 to discuss the economy. Obama and Vice-President Joe Biden wanted to do something big and bold: a "moon shoot." Some of the ideas discussed included a high-speed rail system and a smart grid, but White House Budget Director Peter Orszag said the barrier was not the money. The primary barrier was the overlapping jurisdictions and getting enough cooperation between the parties. Indeed, the reaction on Capitol Hill was one of disbelief. High-speed rail and smart grids were tabled, for now.

Two of the primary architects of ARRA were Christine Romer, University of California at Berkeley economics professor, and economist Jared Bernstein. Romer was concerned about striking the right balance between doing too much and doing too little with a stimulus plan. However, House Appropriations Committee Chairman David Obey, whose tenure in Washington dated back to the Lyndon Johnson administration, pushed for a package well over a trillion dollars. When asked by Chief of Staff Rahm Emanuel if a price tag that big might not scare the American public, Obey said, "Rahm, you will need that shock value so that people understand how serious the problem is."

In order to get ARRA passed, Obama would have to get the support of Congress on the amount of money spent and what it would be spent on. Democratic Congressman James Clyburn from South Carolina said that one trillion was the invisible barrier for Congress. "People got afraid of doing anything over a trillion dollars," he said.

After several days of back and forth discussion and negotiations on the details, including Obama's meeting with House and Senate Republicans on Capitol Hill – a very unusual move for a president – the House of Representatives passed ARRA on February 13, 2009. The final tally was 246 in favor, 183 opposed, with seven Democrats and every Republican representative voting against it. Later that night, ARRA, which came with a cost of $787 billion that was outlined in a 1,071-page document, passed the Senate 60 – 38.

The Goals of ARRA

There were three primary goals of ARRA:

1. Create new jobs and retain the jobs that already existed.
2. Stimulate economic activity in the short term while putting money toward long-term economic growth.
3. Increase transparency and accountability in government spending.

The purpose of ARRA was not to restore employment or economic indicators to the same levels they were before the recession started. ARRA was also never intended to be a long-term solution to the nation's economic problems. It was intended to be a stimulus, or a jump-start, not a permanent fix.

However, there were instances when the Obama administration gave mixed signals to the American public. On one hand, the president called for patience while millions of Americans continued to struggle to make ends meet. On the other hand, there were countless photo opportunities of Obama and Biden at groundbreaking ceremonies, giving the impression that ARRA was the modern day WPA.

Confusion about what the goals of ARRA were and the lack of clear communication from the federal government helped create the initial impression that the stimulus plan was a failure. Few people were excited about the largest investment in clean energy in history or the new Department of Homeland Security headquarters when their own neighborhood was lined with houses in foreclosure.

How the Money was Spent

The stimulus package was designed to be allocated over a period of ten years, but the majority of the money was supposed to be spent within the first two years. Within the three primary goals, ARRA can be broken down into short-term and long-term expenditures.

Examples of Short-Term Spending

- Tax cuts
- Safety net spending, which refers to government programs such as school lunches, Medicare, and tax credits
- Money for states to close budget gaps
- Infrastructure projects, such as highways, bridges, airports, and utilities

Examples of Long-Term Spending:

- Sustainability and clean energy, such as wind and solar

- High-speed rail and other projects to reduce traffic congestion
- Education reform
- Science and research

Immediate Relief

What most Americans wanted to know after ARRA was signed into law was how it was going to help them right now. There were several elements to ARRA's plan for immediate relief.

Tax cuts: During the Bush presidency, American tax payers received rebate checks in 2008 as part of his administration's efforts to stimulate the economy. Individuals received checks of up to $600 and families received up to $1,200. Bush expected Americans to use the checks to make purchases, but rather than spending them on retail products, many people used the rebate checks to pay bills or stashed them in savings accounts.

This set the stage for confusion when, in 2009, ARRA cut taxes by $400 for individuals and $800 for families by reducing withholding of taxes through payroll. The amount of extra money per paycheck was so small, many people did not even realize they were getting it. Therefore, many people thought they were not getting a tax cut, although it amounted to approximately $116 billion in reduced tax revenue for the federal government. This was replaced by the Payroll Tax Holiday in 2011, which reduced the amount of Social Security tax withheld from paychecks, as well as reduced the self-employment tax. For families making $60,000 per year, the 2011 tax cut amounted to about $1,000.

Tax credits: A tax credit can be taken on income tax returns. One of the largest tax credits from ARRA went to first-time homebuyers. From 2009 through April 2010, new homebuyers or people who had not owned a home for at least three years were eligible for a tax credit of 10 percent of the purchase price of the home, up to $8,000. This was intended to not only to put more money in their pockets to make major purchases such as appliances and furniture, but also as an incentive to spur lagging home sales. By this point in the recession, home sales were dropping at nearly 20 percent per year. Approximately 2.3 million people utilized the tax credit, which cost the government about $16.2 billion.

ARRA also provided up to a $2,500 tax credit for college tuition and related expenses in 2009 and 2010, as well as made it easier for the working poor to earn the child tax credit. The earned-income tax credit for families earning a low to moderate wage and having at least three children was also expanded to $5,657. The credits were extended through the 2012 tax year.

Unemployment benefits: Millions of Americans found themselves receiving unemployment benefits – many for the first time in their lives – during the recession. According to the Department of Labor (DOL), more than 4.8 million Americans were receiving unemployment benefits at the end of January 2009. This was a 78 percent increase over 2008 and the highest rate of Americans on unemployment since the DOL began keeping records in 1967.

What some taxpayers did not realize was that unemployment benefits are considered taxable income. ARRA eliminated the taxes on the first $2,400 of that benefit through the 2009 tax year, as well as temporarily increased the monthly benefit by $25. In addition, access to unemployment benefits was extended for another 33 weeks if the first 26 weeks of benefits was exhausted. The cost for expansion of unemployment benefits totaled just under $61 billion.

COBRA: One of the major concerns that unemployed Americans face is health care, since health care is so often tied to jobs. The Consolidated Omnibus Budget Reconciliation Act (COBRA) can provide continued health care for up to 18 months. However, COBRA is often expensive, as the former employee has to pay the entire insurance premium. ARRA provided a 65 percent subsidy for COBRA payments for eligible workers laid off between September 1, 2008 and December 31, 2009. Expanding COBRA cost the government approximately $3.7 billion.

Sales tax on new cars: Taxpayers who purchased a new car, motorcycle, light truck, or motor home by December 31, 2009 were potentially eligible for a federal tax deduction on the state and local sales taxes. This applied to vehicles costing less than $49,500. As an example, a new car that cost $20,000 would have resulted in a sales tax deduction of approximately $2,000.

Social security and pensions: Americans receiving social security benefits, railroad retirees, and military veterans all were eligible to receive an extra payment of $250 in 2009. This included recipients of Supplemental Security Income (SSI), the benefit paid to disabled adults and children with limited sources of other income.

Allocations for Infrastructure

Approximately $80 billion of the stimulus plan, or one-tenth of the total allotment, was allocated for what was loosely defined as infrastructure. This included:

- $46 billion for transportation and mass transit
- $31 billion for federal building renovation and modernization
- $6 billion for water projects

The buzzword that began to surround construction projects vying for ARRA dollars was "shovel-ready," implying that the project had all of its permits and was ready to go once funding was received. Obama routinely used the phrase in reference to plans to rebuild the nation's "crumbling infrastructure." Grabell argues in "Money Well Spent?" that this created "images of blue-collar workers heading out to the heartland with sledgehammers and pickaxes over their shoulders," reminiscent of the New Deal era of the Great Depression. However, it was months before most of the infrastructure projects got underway, and they had little immediate impact on the nation's unemployment problem.

OVER FIVE BILLION DOLLARS WAS ALLOCATED FOR THE MODERNIZATION OF FEDERAL BUILDINGS, WHICH included improvements such as upgrading windows and electrical systems, heating and cooling systems, and thermal insulation, designed to create significant energy savings. For example, the improvements to the federal office building and courthouse in Denver, Colorado were expected to reduce energy usage by a whopping 80 percent.

Education Reform

Education reform received approximately $100 billion. The payout breakdown was $54 billion to states and school districts to fund educational programs and teacher salaries, $21 billion to build new schools and modernize existing ones, $13 billion for Head Start, and $12 billion for special education programs and job training for Americans with disabilities. Another $17 billion was allocated for Pell Grants for college students who otherwise could not afford college.

From the educational perspective, the primary point of the stimulus package was to save jobs and address underperforming schools and school districts. Over $4 billion was issued through the Race to the Top, a competitive grant program that rewards schools for creating innovate learning environments. However, of the 12 states that were awarded funding in the first year of the grant, nine were behind schedule as of January 2012. Another three – New York, Florida, and Hawaii – were in danger of losing their funding.

The impact of this has long-term effects, as it instills doubt that this type of reform works. Education Secretary Arne Duncan said after the news about New York's problems became known, "Backtracking on reform commitments could cost the state hundreds of millions of dollars for improving New York schools," and it "not only impedes Race to the Top but could threaten other key reform initiatives."

Small Businesses

Big corporations and businesses often make splashier headlines, but small businesses are just as important in driving the American economy. According to the Small Business Administration (SBA), two out of three new jobs are created by small businesses. By allocating $54 billion in the stimulus plan to small businesses in loans, credit lines, and tax deductions, the Obama administration hoped that they would have the resources and the incentive to generate great products and services, while also creating jobs. Two years later, the 2011 federal budget included another $64 billion to extend several of the ARRA programs geared toward small businesses, including increasing the SBA loan limit from $3 million to $5 million. While these provisions are not all solely for small businesses, they all applied to small businesses. The initial stimulus package included a special depreciation tax, tax credits for hiring students, veterans, and youth, and a cut in capital gains taxes.

Health Care

ARRA provided approximately $138 billion for the expansion of health care, not only to support the health of taxpayers and their families, but because health care is one of the largest and fastest growing employment industries in the country. Money set aside for health care was not just for health services, but also for improving information technology and promoting research. In addition to the $10 billion in the stimulus plan for modernization of research facilities, the plan included the following elements:

Medicaid: ARRA set aside $87 billion to states in matching funds for support in paying Medicaid, the country's health care program for uninsured, low-income individuals and families. Typically during a recession, the cost of Medicaid goes up because more people lose their health insurance during a faltering economy. At the same time, states are losing revenue, making it more difficult for them to assist those in need. The Kaiser Commission on Medicaid and the Uninsured reported in 2011 that in 2010, the number of Americans receiving Medicaid assistance went above 50 million for the first time in history.

Military hospitals: The stimulus plan allowed for $4 billion to construct or improve military hospitals.

Information technology: Improved information technology is not just a convenience. It can save lives. Hospitals and other medical facilities that have quick access to accurate information can better serve their patients and offer better medical care. Seventeen billion dollars was set aside for the modernization of health information technology systems.

National Institute of Health (NIH): The NIH is one of the world's most renowned medical research facilities. It is overseen by the Department of Health and Human Services. As of May 2012, just under $9 billion of the $10 billion allocated for NIH had been spent on 21,700 projects across every state, Washington, D.C., Guam, and Puerto Rico. Examples of these projects range from training Meals on Wheels volunteers to teach elderly citizens how to better communicate with health care providers, to studying breast cancer and Alzheimer's Disease. A positive effect of initiating more research projects is not just the data collected, but putting scientists and other researchers to work.

Transparency

Transparency refers to openly communicating about decisions that affect other people. One of the goals of ARRA was the promise to increase the transparency of the federal government and communicate more openly about where the stimulus package dollars were being spent.

Accountability for government spending on this scale was vital. There were already requirements for reporting in place due to an act passed by Congress in 2006, but it was never enforced. Obama could not take any chances with ARRA. The stimulus package could not work and the credibility of the Obama administration would have been severely damaged by any hints of fraud, kickbacks, or similar misuse of funds. As a result, the level of accountability required of the states and localities receiving stimulus dollars was unprecedented.

Federal reports on ARRA funds required that 99 fields of information be completed, which included general summaries and descriptions of the projects, as well as itemized lists of expenditures. Data was also required from contractors and subcontractors working on ARRA-funded projects. Rather than report directly to the agency issuing the funding, those receiving stimulus dollars were required to report the details of their spending to the website FederalReporting.gov.

Fraud and misuse of funds was a fear in issuing a stimulus plan of this magnitude. To combat that, Earl Devaney, former inspector general for the Interior Department, worked with 28 inspectors general from other government agencies to develop the Recovery Operations Center. At a cost of approximately $5 million, 17 analysts use technology commonly utilized in law enforcement and intelligence to track ARRA funding and its recipients. The result was, for the first time in the nation's history, a central database of federal contractor information, available to the country's 29 inspectors general.

For public information, the federal government developed the website Recovery.gov, which "provides easy access to data related to Recovery Act spending and allows for the reporting of potential fraud, waste, and abuse." The website allows anyone to track spending and look up the progress of projects. This provides a layer of accountability for communities to not only follow through on spending money the way it was intended to be spent, but helps ensure that contracts were awarded ethically.

Initially, there was minimal information available on Recovery.gov and much of the information that was there was written in cryptic, government code that meant little to the average citizen. However, as the stimulus money was spent, projects launched and then completed, reports began to be filed and the website became more functional and robust. The information available there is free from political commentary on whether or not the projects are good, bad, necessary, or unnecessary. It is factual information on the flow of money.

With all of the debate about the wisdom and economic results of ARRA, there is little debate about the impact the act had on government transparency. Leaders on both sides of the political aisle can agree that ARRA did more to promote transparency in government spending than any recent bill, law, or similar piece of legislation.

Results: Did the Stimulus Plan Work?

Before the ink was dry on ARRA, everyone had a variation of the same question: is it going to work? Susie Gharib, an anchor on PBS's Nightly News Report, had that question for Warren Buffet days after the stimulus plan was signed into law. Buffet, one of the world's richest men and viewed by many to be the most successful investor in the 20th century, said, "Nobody knows."

The truth was that nobody did know. There were bold predictions of success from the Democrats and ominous warnings of failure from the Republicans. Buffet did have other wise words for the days ahead, though. "...If you think that he [Obama] can turn things around in a month or three months or six months and there's going to be some magical transformation since he took office on the 20th, that can't happen ..."

And it didn't. When all was said and done, 270,000 recipients were awarded stimulus dollars, but an anxious nation was quick to initially declare ARRA a failure. On one hand, many said it cost too much, yet on the other hand, those same critics said it did too little to impact the economy.

Job loss and, ultimately, job gains are a large yardstick by which the success or failure of ARRA is measured. For better or worse, the Obama administration set it up that way by promising that the country would not go above eight percent unemployment if ARRA was passed. Ironically, Christine Romer gave little thought to the graph that she included in her report on what the stimulus plan could mean for the future of employment in the United States. She included it because the Obama transition team thought it would be better to have a visual aid.

However, before the report was published, Romer asked her husband, also an economist, to review it. He pointed out that including the eight percent figure on the graph could be big mistake. "Now you know you're breaking an implicit rule. You don't put down a number like the employment rate because it's easy to turn out to be wrong," he said. Romer replied, "If the unemployment rate is 10 percent, we have much bigger problems than that I didn't predict it correctly." Looking back, Romer said she made an error not with her prediction, but by not emphasizing more that the figures she presented had a "significant margin of error."

That 8 percent figure is one cited repeatedly by critics of the plan, particularly when the national unemployment rate soared as high as 10.2 percent in November 2009. Ultimately, though, Romer and Bernstein's predictions may not have been so far off the mark. They said that without a stimulus package, the unemployment rate would be about two percentage points higher than with one. Moody's economist, Mark Zandi, predicted that without a stimulus package, the unemployment rate could get as high as 11 percent. Some forecasted an unemployment rate as high as 12 percent. Therefore, some could argue that ARRA did keep the unemployment rate from going as high as it could have potentially gone.

Had the Obama administration communicated that a lag in unemployment rates following a stimulus is typical, perhaps the American public would have been more forgiving. A six-month lag in unemployment after economic growth can be expected, according to many economists, because it takes time for the money that is injected into the economy to have an effect, and it takes even more time for that to translate into hiring.

According to the Bureau of Labor Statistics, the private sector added jobs every month between March 2010 and January 2012. Over the last three months of 2011, an average of 245,000 new jobs were added each month. The month that Obama took office, the economy was losing nearly 20,000 jobs every day. By January 2012, the unemployment rate was at 8.3 percent and by April 2012, it was 8.1 percent.

Zandi and fellow economist Alan Blinder of Princeton University, former Federal Reserve vice-chairman, estimated that ARRA, combined with Obama's other economic policies, added 2.7 million jobs to the workforce. The Congressional Budget Office (CBO), the non-partisan federal agency charged with reviewing congressional budgets, reported in February 2012 that the impact of ARRA peaked in the third fiscal quarter of 2010 when it was responsible for saving and adding a combined 3.6 million jobs. Zandi and economists from Macroeconomic Advisers and IHS/Global Insight estimated that in the second quarter of 2011, ARRA added between about 2.1 million and 2.6 million jobs.

According to the CBO, ARRA was also responsible for increasing worker hours into 2011, as many employees saw their hours reduced during the recession. Without ARRA, the CBO reports, more workers would have been reduced to part-time status or not had the opportunity to work overtime. In all, nonpartisan economic forecasters credit ARRA with the creation and retention of more than two million jobs.

Six months after it was signed into law, a USA Today/Gallup poll revealed that 57 percent of adults claimed that the stimulus plan had not only not improved the economy, it had made it worse. Sixty percent of those polled said they doubted that the plan would improve the economy in the future. A mere 18 percent said that their personal financial situation had improved. Republican leaders called it a "flop." John McCain said, ""A lot of it has been spent on ridiculous projects," and his fellow Republican senator from Arizona, Jon Kyl, called for the plan to be halted in July 2009. Meanwhile, President Obama urged Americans to be patient and Democratic Senator Dick Durbin from Illinois said, "It's a two-year plan and we're four months into it."

Fueling the anxiety and predictions of doom for ARRA was the assessment by many that the Obama administration was too slow in spending the stimulus money. For example, Steven Chu, the Department of Energy secretary, said two days after ARRA was signed into law that there would be "a sweeping reorganization of the DOE's dispersal of direct loans, loan guarantees and funding contained in the new recovery legislation." He added, "The goal of the restructuring is to expedite disbursement of money to begin investments in a new energy economy that will put Americans back to work and create millions of new jobs." He promised that 70 percent of the DOE's share of the stimulus plan would be spent by the end of 2010.

That did not happen. In fact, as the calendar turned to 2011, a little under half of the stimulus dollars allocated to the DOE remained in the bank, amounting to about $15 billion still unused. The story was the same across the board. Job retraining programs, weatherizing projects, breaking ground on new roads, and countless other programs and projects were delayed by the lack of expediency in getting the money flowing.

When the money did begin to reach its intended recipients and projects were underway, the question changed from "will it work" to "did it work?" The answer is still not a definitive "yes" or "no." Even economists cannot unanimously agree. In February 2012, the Booth School of Business at the University of Chicago asked a panel of economic experts representing various political views about ARRA. Eight of the 10 said the stimulus plan did contribute to lower unemployment by the end of 2010 and most said it was worth the cost, but there were still vocal opponents on the panel.

In many respects, answering the question about whether or not ARRA worked depends on how success or failure is defined. It also depends on who you ask because Republicans are, on the whole, extremely reluctant to admit anything that President Obama does is a success. The only way to really know if ARRA worked is to compare it to what *would* have happened to the American economy if no stimulus plan had been implemented which, again, is unknowable. Economists can make guesses and have done so, but nobody really knows for certain.

What is known is that after ARRA was signed into law, the recession ended four months later. Unemployment rates dropped. The GDP, the equivalent of taking the country's financial temperature, went up from -4.9 percent in March 2009 to +5.0 percent by the end of the year. The Dow Industrial Average, which is the index of stock prices of 30 of the biggest and most influential companies in the U.S and widely considered to be another strong indicator of the health of the American economy, had also risen to 10,428 by the end of the fourth quarter. In March it had fallen down to 6,547 and the Dow lost 20 percent of its value in just six weeks. The economy began to recover. Whether or not ARRA should be credited for these economic events is, and will likely remain, open to interpretation.

Chapter 3: Obama and the Housing Crisis

The beginning of the recession that gripped the economy as Obama took office in January 2009 can be traced back several years earlier, during George W Bush's presidency. Millions were living the American dream of home ownership, long portrayed as the symbol of success. Bush urged federal and private lenders to create ways for more and more people to buy houses, making home ownership a reality for millions of people who may not have otherwise thought it was possible. As interest rates dropped below 6 percent, new home sales reached record levels in 2002, with an estimated 969,000 homes purchased.

Meanwhile, the demand for housing was on the rise, driving up the value of houses and creating an illusion of wealth. Consumers took advantage of the low interest rates and refinanced their mortgages, taking cash out of their homes for anything from home repairs to furniture, cars, or vacations. For many, money was easy to get and their houses became similar to ATM machines. Each drop in interest rates led to more refinancing and more cash taken out.

As the housing market boomed, more banks and lenders wanted to cash in and targeted potential buyers who might not otherwise qualify, either due to lack of cash for a down-payment or poor credit. These risky loans, called subprime loans, made many people home owners. It was not unusual for a mortgage to be granted with no money down and no documented source of income.

By 2006, there were signs that the housing bubble was going to burst. In the first quarter of the year, the median price of a home in the U.S. had dropped 3.3 percent from the previous quarter. The subprime mortgages were the first to falter. Putting people in houses that they could not afford, especially when mortgages with adjustable interest rates reset and pushed up the cost of monthly payments, led to lenders not getting their money back. Faced with increased payments, sometimes hundreds of dollars more than their original payment, millions of Americans began to fall behind on their mortgages

When the housing bubble did burst, millions of homeowners either lost their homes to foreclosure or were stuck in homes that they could not sell because they were no longer worth the purchase price. The ramifications were felt in bank closures, the plunging stock market, and the loss of jobs. With rising unemployment, homeowners with conventional loans were now also losing their homes to foreclosure.

An avalanche of foreclosures began in 2008 that would not begin to subside for three more years. Between 2008 and 2011, four million homes in the U.S. were lost to foreclosure. The Board of Governors for the Federal Reserve estimates that the collapse of the housing market was responsible for a $7 trillion decline in household wealth in the U.S. As was the case with the economy as a whole, Obama's election came with the expectation that he make the housing crisis a top priority.

Making Home Affordable (MHA)

Obama unveiled his first mortgage program within weeks of taking office in January 2009. Using $50 billion from TARP funds, Making Home Affordable (MHA) was initiated in March. MHA contained two components, the Home Affordable Mortgage Program (HAMP) and Home Affordable Refinance Program (HARP). HAMP was targeted to homeowners with subprime mortgages, which represented a smaller contingent of people having trouble paying back their home loan. The criteria for eligibility resulted in criticism that too many homeowners could not be helped with this program, as it provided assistance only on first mortgages that represented more than 31 percent of monthly income.

HAMP was also a voluntary program for mortgage servicers, who did not have to participate. It did nothing to address second mortgages, nor did it forgive debt and help those with negative equity in their homes. The Senate blocked a measure that would have allowed bankruptcy judges to restructure mortgage payments on primary residences.

The Obama administration promised to aid four million borrowers with HAMP, but three years later, only 900,000 people had received assistance from the program. While not an insignificant number, it fell far short of projections. HAMP was expanded in 2012 to increase the incentives for lenders to forgive a portion of a mortgage. For example, if a home is worth $150,000 but the mortgage is $200,000, lenders who forgive the $50,000 will be reimbursed for half of that amount by the federal government. The total cost to American taxpayers is estimated at $2.1 billion, according to the Federal Housing Finance Agency.

Home Affordable Refinance Program (HARP)

HARP allowed eligible homeowners to refinance their mortgages through Fannie Mae and Freddie Mac. Some homeowners were frustrated with the fact that an appraisal was required and they could only refinance up to 105 percent of their home value. This left many people with underwater mortgages, or mortgages with balances higher than their home's value, with no assistance. Later, that was expanded to 125 percent of home value, but it still left much in the hands of appraisers.

In March 2012, a revamped version of HARP, called HARP 2.0, was implemented and extended through 2013. The new version eliminated the need for an appraisal and the loan-to-value ratio. These changes showed some success through May 2012. Over 180,000 loans were refinanced under HARP 2.0, twice as many as the 93,000 loans refinanced under HARP in the fourth quarter of 2011. Also, more people who were seriously underwater were being helped, with 41,000 loans above 105 percent of the home's value being refinanced in the first quarter of 2012, compared to 13,000 in the final quarter of 2011.

Dodd-Frank Wall Street Reform and Protection Act

Congress passed this broad piece of legislation in July 2010 with the intent of preventing a future financial crisis. One result of the act was the development of the Consumer Financial Protection Bureau, which sets rules and examines all regulations related to financial products and services offered to consumers. The law requires that mortgage providers adhere to several rules and changes.

- Requires lenders to ensure that borrowers can repay loans

- Prohibits lenders from using financial incentives to encourage borrowers to accept more expensive loans
- Limits pre-payment penalties on fixed mortgages and eliminates them on adjustable-rate and sub-prime loans
- Limits late fees on late payments
- Fines mortgage servicers for irresponsible lending practices
- Provides more financial counseling for prospective home buyers

Other Measures

HAMP and HARP are the most discussed programs in Obama's efforts to mitigate the housing crisis, but they are not the only ones.

Principal Reduction Alternative Program:
Participating mortgage services may offer eligible homeowners a reduction in the total amount owed on their home. The hope is that reducing the principal will increase the likelihood of being repaid.

Home Affordable Foreclosures Alternative: This assists homeowners who can no longer pay their mortgage by helping them short-sale, or sell the home for less than is owed, or initiate a Deed in Lieu of Foreclosure, which permits the home owner to give the title back to the lender.

Hardest Hit Fund: This $7.6 billion was provided to the District of Columbia and 18 states that were most affected by the housing crisis. The funds were given to help those areas develop their own foreclosure prevention programs.

Home Affordable Unemployment Program: This program allowed unemployed HAMP participants to receive forbearance, or a temporary delay in making payments, for up to 12 months

Robo-signing Settlement: Robo-signing is the term given to the practice of automatically signing off on mortgage papers without actually reviewing them for accuracy. Federal and state agencies reached a settlement totaling $25 billion with the five largest mortgage services in the U.S. These funds could help eligible borrowers have the balance of their mortgages reduced by as much as $150,000.

Results of Mortgage Reform

President Obama did fall short of his goals in addressing the housing crisis, but experts say that it is not likely he could have done much to immediately stabilize the market. Ed Jacob, executive director of the non-profit organization Neighborhood Housing Services of Chicago, said in January 2012, "I don't think anyone could have done anything to stabilize the housing market… This housing market was in far worse shape than anyone knew."

Obama was also hampered by disagreements with Congress on how to address unemployment, which remains a key component to steadying the housing market. Without jobs and a reliable income, most Americans cannot purchase houses. Gabriel Stuart, the director of the Ziman Center for Real Estate at UCLA said, "Obama was in many ways hemmed in as to effectively and positively affect the housing crisis…the economy was moving under their feet."

By June 2012, home equity still accounted for the lowest share of net wealth in the U.S. since 1945. However, the Joint Center for Housing Studies at Harvard University reported that there were signs of recovery in the first quarter of 2012.

- There was a 5.2 percent increase from the previous years in existing home sales of single-family homes and condos.

- Sales of newly built homes were up 16.7 percent from 2011.
- Single-family home permits increased 16.9 percent from the previous year.

Struggles remain, though. The number of mortgages that were delinquent by 90 days or more in the first quarter of 2012 was 7 percent, significantly higher than the average of 1.7 percent during the 1990s. More than two million homes were still in the foreclosure process in early 2012 and some states still had a large number of homeowners with negative equity. Nevada had a rate of 61 percent of underwater mortgages and 48 percent of Arizona homeowners owed more than their houses were worth.

Chapter 4: Obama and the Auto Bailout

As the American economy was in crisis in 2008, no industry was in danger of demise more than automobile manufacturing. General Motors (GM) and Chrysler both faced bankruptcy and even though Ford did not, the company still understood that the death of its competitors would seriously damage the auto industry as a whole. In December 2008, the so-called "Big 3" of the auto world asked the federal government for $34 billion to avoid bankruptcy and the potential of ceasing operations.

The auto industry crisis had been building over time and was the result of several factors. In the late 1990s, sport utility vehicles (SUVs) and trucks were responsible for half of the American car market. Auto manufacturers were happy to oblige as these vehicles offered them the largest profit margins. However, as energy prices increased, the demand for large vehicles dropped. Consumers wanted cars with smaller gas tanks that offered greater fuel efficiency. The Big 3 was unprepared for this shift in demand and was not only unable to provide vehicles to rival those from foreign makers such as Toyota and Nissan, they were left with a glut of unwanted vehicles.

Americans also had less money to spend on new vehicles. As the economy faltered, the ability to afford a new car went with it. There was less demand for American automakers' products globally as much of the world was also suffering from a downturn in the economy. The Big 3 was already suffering from a negative perception about their product. Foreign automakers had been dominating the market for many years as American consumers were turned off by what many viewed as inferior vehicles. In 1962, GM had over 50 percent of the new vehicle market. By 2007, the company's share had dwindled to 23 percent.

Both George W Bush and Barack Obama received significant opposition to an auto industry bailout. A CNN poll in December 2008 showed that 61 percent of those polled were against it. By the time Obama took office, that number was up to 72 percent. The prevailing attitude among many of the opponents was that the auto industry was in an economic mess because of its flawed business model. By simply writing a check, there would be no incentive to change its ways. Among the critics of the bailout was Mitt Romney, the former governor of Massachusetts and a 2008 and 2012 Republican candidate for president. He famously wrote an op-ed piece for "The New York Times" in November 2008 titled "Let Detroit Go Bankrupt" that proclaimed, "you can kiss the American auto industry goodbye" if automakers received a bailout.

Neither Bush nor Obama were prepared to allow the auto industry to fail. Prior to the bailout, automakers were responsible for 3.6 percent of the nation's GDP, amounting to over $500 billion. Bush's Council of Economic Advisors estimated that if U.S. automakers failed and its workers were laid off, it would result in a 1 percent drop in the real GDP and 1.1 million workers would lose their jobs. A failure in the auto industry would also lead to a decrease in the need for materials needed to manufacture cars, such as steel and glass, and add a massive influx of workers in need of jobs at a time when jobs were difficult to find.

Presidential Response to the Crisis

On December 19, 2008, Bush announced that GM and Chrysler would receive $13.4 billion from the Troubled Asset Relief Program, with Chrysler eligible for another $4 billion when Congress made the second half of the TARP funds available. In exchange, the companies had until March 31 to produce a plan to show how they would fix their financial problems, get out of debt, and start to show a profit again.

Ford was in better financial condition than GM and Chrysler because it had raised $24.5 billion by mortgaging its assets in 2006. It did not request TARP funds, but it did request a line of credit from the government totaling $9 billion, as well as a $5 billion loan from the Depart of Energy. Ford's primary concern was losing a competitive edge with GM and Chrysler, who were set to benefit from the government bailout. One of Ford's promises to the government was to speed up the production of alternative fuel vehicles.

Both GM and Ford agreed to reduce the number of brands in production, resulting in Ford selling off Volvo. The CEOs of the Big 3 – Chrysler's Robert Nardelli, GM CEO Rick Wagoner, and Ford CEO Alan Mulally – all agreed to work for the salary of $1 during the year after the bailout and sell their corporate jets. The companies also agreed to allow the federal government access to their bookkeeping records and give the feds the power to veto transactions over $100 million.

Although the bailout began in the Bush administration, Obama provided the majority of the $85 billion that the automakers eventually received. When he received their viability plans in March 2009, he rejected them. Instead, he put GM and Chrysler into managed bankruptcy plans, which allowed the companies to receive more funding and restructure their operations.

Results of the Auto Bailout

President Bush and, later, President Obama were in a position where either the government intervened or the auto industry in the U.S. would have closed its doors. Estimates are that at least one million jobs would have been lost. Despite remarks from critics such as former-Governor Romney that private funds should have been used, there were no private funds available at that time. Credit lines were frozen and there was no private entity willing or able to act to save the Big 3.

Steven Rattner, who led the bailout for the Obama administration, said in 2012 that the government would have rather not become involved, but top administrators felt like there was little choice. Rattner said, "There's no question what would have happened. Chrysler and General Motors would have run out of cash…" Bankruptcy expert Harvey R. Miller, who advised both GM and the Lehman Brothers through their bankruptcies, said that without government intervention, it was "very unlikely" that the GM and Chrysler would have survived without a bailout and that the Treasury Department was the only entity capable of doing it.

Within three years of the bailout, the auto industry had righted itself. In 2011, all of the Big 3 had improved their markets shares and were making profits. Ford reported $2 million in sales in 2011 for the first time since 2007. In January 2012, GM reclaimed the position as the bestselling automaker in the world, supplanting Toyota. Workers were rehired and found a new, more streamlined environment, similar to how automakers in Japan and Germany operate.

The benchmark for healthy sales figures from the automakers in Detroit is 15 million sales in a year. In 2011, automakers sold 12.8 million cars and trucks. By March 2012, estimates were that 15.1 million vehicles would be sold, with buyers spending almost $2,000 more per car than the previous year.

In 2011, Chrysler paid back $11.2 billion of the $12.5 it received from the government. However, government officials stated from the beginning that they did not expect to get all of the money back. Treasury Secretary Timothy Geithner said in 2011, "We didn't do this to maximize return. We did it to save jobs." The federal government also received $60 million from Fiat when the Italian automaker agreed to buy the Treasury's 6 percent stake in Chrysler. GM repaid about half of the $50 billion it received and the government maintained about 500 million shared in the company as of 2012. When Dan Akerson, who took over as CEO of Chrysler in 2010, was asked if Obama saved GM he said, "At the risk of alienating a whole lot of potential customers, I would say the Obama administration did a good job."

Chapter 5: Obama and Sustainability

Lyndon Baines Johnson may have signed more environmental bills into law during his term in office, but Barack Obama has arguably created more of a buzz about sustainability and "green" business than any president in history. Before he was even a candidate for president, Obama wrote of the need for alternative energy in his 2006 book, "The Audacity of Hope." He wrote that government investment in alternative energy was one key element to the prevention of jobs being shipped overseas and to restoring the economy. Therefore, even with domestic crude oil production at an 8-year high in 2012, nobody should be surprised to see sustainability and renewable energy be part of his on-going economic policy.

Investment in Renewable Energy

According to the National Venture Capital Association, more than $4 billion was invested in renewable energy, including solar and wind power, in 2008. The Obama administration jumped on this bandwagon soon after Obama took office and gave over $44 billion in loans, subsidies, and tax incentives to clean technology between 2009 and 2011.

In his State of the Union address in January 2012, Obama announced that the U.S. Navy would be purchasing up to a gigawatt of alternative energy by 2020, which is enough to power 250,000 homes a year. Ray Mabus, secretary of the Navy, said that not only will this help cut down on fuel purchases from volatile areas of the world, it will save money. He pointed out that the USS Makin Island operates using a hybrid drive, which saved $2 million in fuel costs on its initial voyage and has the potential to save a billion dollars in fuel costs over the life of the ship.

Cited by The New York Times as the largest energy bill in U.S. history, Obama also allocated $70 billion of ARRA to renewable energy programs and research. Programs and tax credits receiving funding from the stimulus package include the following:

Energy improvement tax credit: The stimulus plan was not the first attempt to reward homeowners for implementing energy improvements. A tax credit was created in 2005, but it was too complex for many taxpayers to understand and the payoff was not worth it. ARRA eliminated the $500 lifetime cap and allowed for a tax credit of up to $1,500 for energy improvements such as solar energy systems, geothermal heat pumps, and residential wind turbines. This amounted to a credit of 30 percent of the cost with no upper limit through 2016.

Weatherization for low-income families: $5 billion was allocated for the weatherization of homes for low-income families, intended to save on energy costs and improve the health of those living in the home. For a family of four, the annual income limit was just over $58,000. Renters could participate if they could secure approval from their landlords. Weatherization included replacing energy-inefficient appliances, changing out broken doors and windows, repairing holes and sealing drafts, and educating the residents about efficient energy usage.

The Innovative Technology and Loan Guarantee Program: This program provided $6 billion for companies and business for "cleantech" projects, or projects that use technology that produce lower pollution and greenhouse gasses. The program also allowed the Department of Energy (DOE) to offer loan guarantees of up to 80 percent of the cost of the project.

Renewable energy tax credit: The stimulus plan provided $2.3 billion in tax credits to support renewable energy. Companies involved in the development of renewable energy, including solar, wind, geothermal, water, and biomass, were eligible for a 30 percent investment tax credit.

Research and development tax credit: ARRA provided a 20 percent research and development tax credit through the 2010 tax year for research in fields including renewable energy, battery technology, and fuel cells. This was intended to support alternative energy products that were not yet available on the commercial market, but rather were still in the testing phase.

Electric Cars

Grants totaling over $2 billion were awarded to fund 48 projects focused on advanced battery and electric drive projects. Before ARRA, an electric car cost about $100,000 in the United States. Even if you could afford one, chances were you could not drive far because charging stations were few and far between. In fact, there were only 500 charging stations in the entire country, compared to the well over 100,000 gas stations dotting the roads and highways in the U.S.

By December 2010, there were two mass-produced electric cars available to American drivers. The Nissan Leaf, which started at $33,000, ran solely on electricity and could go 100 miles between charges. Thanks to $1.4 billion from the Energy Department, the Nissan plant in Smyrna, Tennessee was renovated so that it could manufacture these cars. General Motors in Detroit received $400 million to help build the Volt, a hybrid with a starting price of about $40,00 that could go 40 miles before the gasoline engine took over.

The Results

The indicator for success that most people look to when assessing Obama's focus on renewable energy is jobs. He made lofty promises during his campaign that an investment in clean technology would not only help the environment, it would create jobs. He boldly predicted five million jobs would be added over 10 years, although it is not clear what information Obama used to come up with that figure. ARRA provided $500 million for training to prepare a workforce to work in energy efficiency and renewable energy. Much talk surrounded these primarily blue-collar jobs in career paths such as solar panel installers and windmill technicians.

Obama's focus on sustainability raised high hopes at colleges and universities, too. Arizona State University opened the School of Sustainability in 2007. ASU touted its program as the first in the world to offer undergraduate and graduate degrees in sustainability, pointing toward the emphasis on renewable energy in the stimulus plan as proof that their program was preparing the job force of the future.

Those jobs have been slow to materialize. The Brookings Institution reported that between 2003 and 2010, less than 10,000 jobs in the renewable energy field had been created. Only one out of 10 people trained with ARRA funds had jobs as of January 2010. However, one barrier to "green job" growth was that the grant was awarded at a time when few sectors were hiring. The discussion around green jobs has also been muddled by the confusion about what makes a job "green" and whether there really is a large market for them.

Obama's policies have also been stymied, to a degree, by the government's investment in Solyndra, a solar panel manufacturer and the first company to receive a federally guaranteed loan from the stimulus plan in 2009. George W Bush had already expressed his support of the loan guarantee program before he left office, and Solyndra had a loan application pending when Obama took office. It was the Obama administration that finalized the loan and the Bay Area manufacturer was used by Obama as a shining example of the type of company – and jobs – that the stimulus plan was intended to create. "The true engine of economic growth will always be companies like Solyndra," Obama said from company headquarters in May 2010.

However, as the economy faltered, venture capitalists stopped funding clean technology and companies began to rely more on the federal government. The Obama administration used federal dollars to compensate for the lack of investors, also keeping in mind Obama's campaign promise to address climate change. Solyndra used its $535 million loan to fund the construction of a new plant in Fremont, California. Meanwhile, Chinese solar panel manufacturers were developing methods to build the panels more cheaply.

By August 2011, Solyndra was bankrupt, 1,500 workers were laid off, and pundits were questioning Obama's connections to one of the company's primary investors. Solyndra not only went from an example of everything that was right with the stimulus to everything that was wrong, but Obama's focus on renewable energy was also questioned.

Yet there have been successes, too. Copper Mountain Solar in Nevada is the biggest solar energy producer in the country and was partially financed by $40 million in federal investment tax credits. Both Democrats and Republicans in Nevada have praised the plant as a positive example of how solar power can be harnessed and turned into energy. The Ivanpah solar power plant in the Mohave Desert in California has used a $1.6 billion loan guarantee from the government to build the largest concentrated solar power project in the world, with a capacity of 392 megawatts. When complete, it will generate enough energy to power nearly 87,000 homes a year. The plant was one-third complete as of June 2012 and had over 1,700 employees.

Chapter 6: Conclusion

President Barack Obama will forever be judged by the successes and failures of the American Recovery and Reinvestment Act and subsequent measures he took in an attempt to rescue America's economy from a malaise not seen since the Great Depression. ARRA receives most of the attention because it was not only the first major legislation of his administration – the bill was signed before he had even been president for a month – but because of the cost and what it was intended to do.

There are many challenges in assessing the decisions and policies of a current president, particularly when they are linked to the economy. Determining success or failure often requires time. Those who hoped for employment and the economy as a whole to be restored to pre-recession conditions will remain disappointed, but that was not the intent of the stimulus plan. The intent was to stop the bleeding.

The short answer to whether or not the economy improved after ARRA was implemented is "yes." Three months after ARRA was passed, the recession ended. The GDP improved within months. After dropping a startling 6.9 percent in the first quarter of 2009, it grew by 1.6 percent in the third quarter. After a lag, unemployment began to fall and both the government and the private sector added millions of jobs.

Unfortunately, even if the stimulus plan had been the best piece of economic legislation ever brought forth to the American people, there would be more than a few who would still dismiss it because Obama's name is attached to it. The political climate of the early 21st century is extremely partisan, and this type of division makes compromise and making the country a better place to live and work more difficult. Not a single Republican voted for ARRA, virtually ensuring that not a single Republican can be caught saying anything positive about it.

However, it is hard to put an $800 billion stimulus package into the economy and billions more in the auto industry and mortgage reform and see no impact. Education reform, emphasis on renewable energy, thousands of miles of new roads, hundreds of thousands of improvements to homes, and 3,000 schools in rural America getting connected to the internet are just some of the good things that happened thanks to ARRA.

Despite the critics, Obama's bailout is widely praised for rescuing the American auto industry, which has returned to profitability faster than many expected. The housing market is not healthy, but there are signs of recovery. Green jobs may not have materialized at the rate he projected, but the country is relying less on foreign oil and the government is invested in generating more renewable energy. Obama himself admitted in May 2012 that his administration still had work to do on the economy, offering a grade of "incomplete" when asked to give his own opinion of how the economy was functioning.

However, for further proof of the polarized mood of American politics during Obama's first term, one needs to look no further than the results of a Gallup poll, issued in February 2012. When asked how they would rank Obama against other U.S. presidents in history, the results were split: 38 percent said he would rank as above average or outstanding, while 35 percent said they would rate him as below average or poor. How could Obama be both one of the best and one of the worst presidents in history? As is the case with most of his policies, it may just depend on whom you ask.

About Minute Help

Minute Help Press is building a library of books for people with only minutes to spare. Follow @minutehelp on Twitter to receive the latest information about free and paid publications from Minute Help Press, or visit minutehelp.com

www.ingramcontent.com/pod-product-compliance
Lightning Source LLC
Chambersburg PA
CBHW070128290526
45789CB00005B/2157